Large Print Halloween Adult coloring book for seniors. Easy coloring books for adults relaxation

Big, Bold, and Easy-to-Color Designs for Stress Relief and Relaxation

Hazel Thorne

Chapter 1

Welcome to Your Halloween Coloring Adventure

Welcome to this special Halloween-themed adult coloring book, designed especially for those who love the magic of Halloween and the joy of creativity. This book is created with larger print and bold, high-contrast designs to make coloring more enjoyable and accessible for individuals with low vision, seniors, or anyone who prefers clear, easy-to-see images.

Coloring is a relaxing and therapeutic activity that allows you to unwind, express yourself, and bring beautiful artwork to life. Whether you are a lifelong fan of Halloween or simply looking for a fun way to spend time, this book offers a variety of spooky and charming illustrations to spark your creativity.

Take your time, choose your favorite colors, and enjoy the process of transforming these pages into your own masterpieces.

The Wonderful Benefits of Coloring for Adults

Coloring isn't just for children—it's a relaxing and enjoyable activity for adults of all ages, especially seniors. Whether you're looking for a way to unwind, sharpen your mind, or simply have fun, coloring can be a delightful and rewarding pastime. With large-print designs made especially for those with vision challenges, anyone can experience the joy of bringing images to life with color.

Here are some of the key benefits of coloring:

Relaxation and Stress Relief

Life can be full of worries, but coloring offers a peaceful escape. Research has shown that engaging in creative activities, such as coloring, helps lower stress levels and promotes relaxation. The simple, repetitive motion of filling in a design allows your mind to focus on the present moment, soothing anxious thoughts and creating a calming effect similar to meditation. As you glide your pencil or marker across the page, you may find yourself feeling more at ease, with tension melting away.

Enhancing Focus and Mindfulness

Coloring requires concentration—staying within the lines, choosing colors, and paying attention to small details all engage the brain in a meaningful way. This practice enhances focus, improves attention span, and encourages mindfulness by drawing you into the present moment. Instead of worrying about the past or future, you become fully immersed in the colors and patterns before you. For seniors, practicing mindfulness through coloring can contribute to mental clarity and a greater sense of inner peace.

Cognitive Stimulation and Brain Health

Just like puzzles and reading, coloring is an excellent way to keep the brain engaged and active. Studies suggest that creative activities can help maintain cognitive function and even slow down age-related memory decline. When you color, your brain works to coordinate your hand movements, recall color combinations, and make small creative decisions, all of which help strengthen neural connections. This makes coloring a fantastic tool for keeping the mind sharp while having fun.

Fine Motor Skill Development

As we age, maintaining dexterity in our hands and fingers becomes more important than ever. Coloring can be a gentle but effective way to improve fine motor skills, strengthen hand muscles, and enhance coordination. The act of gripping a coloring pencil and carefully guiding it across the page helps with hand flexibility, making it a wonderful exercise for those dealing with arthritis or reduced mobility. Best of all, it doesn't feel like therapy—it's simply an enjoyable way to express yourself!

Nostalgia, Joy, and the Magic of Halloween

Halloween is a time filled with nostalgia—memories of trick-or-treating, carving pumpkins, spooky decorations, and festive costumes come rushing back. Coloring Halloween-themed images can transport you to the magic of childhood, sparking joy and rekindling cherished moments. Whether it's a grinning jack-o'-lantern, a friendly ghost, or a cozy autumn scene, each page offers a chance to relive fond memories and embrace the playful spirit of the season.

Coloring is a simple pleasure that brings countless benefits, from relaxation and focus to creativity and connection. So, grab your favorite coloring tools, find a cozy spot, and enjoy the wonderful world of coloring—it's never too late to add more color to your life!

Tips for Enjoying Your Coloring Experience

To make the most of your coloring experience, here are a few tips to enhance your enjoyment:

Choosing the Right Coloring Tools

- **Colored Pencils**: Great for blending, shading, and creating detailed effects.

- **Markers**: Provide vibrant, bold colors but may bleed through thinner paper.

- **Gel Pens**: Offer smooth application and are ideal for adding highlights or metallic effects.

- **Crayons**: A great option for those who prefer a softer, easy-to-grip tool.

Using Bold and Bright Colors

For individuals with low vision, using high-contrast colors such as deep blues, bright yellows, and rich oranges can make the images easier to see and more visually appealing. Experimenting with color combinations can also bring an image to life in unexpected ways.

Adding Depth with Shading and Blending

Try layering different shades of the same color to create depth and dimension. For example, using a darker shade on the edges of a pumpkin and a lighter shade in the center can make it look more realistic.

Enhancing the Background

To make your artwork stand out, consider adding a simple background. A soft gray shadow can make objects appear more three-dimensional, while a blue or purple background can give a night-time effect.

Using Different Mediums

Feel free to mix different coloring tools. For instance, you might use colored pencils for fine details and markers for larger areas. Adding a touch of metallic gel pen can create a shimmering effect for magical Halloween elements like stars and moons.

Fun Halloween Trivia and Facts

Adding a bit of Halloween knowledge can make the coloring experience even more engaging. Here are some interesting facts about this spooky holiday:

The History of Halloween

Halloween originated from the ancient Celtic festival of **Samhain**, celebrated over 2,000 years ago. It was believed that on the night of October 31st, the boundary between the living and the dead was at its weakest, allowing spirits to cross over into the world of the living.

Why Do We Carve Pumpkins?

Carving pumpkins, or "jack-o'-lanterns," began as an Irish tradition. People originally carved turnips and placed candles inside them to ward off evil spirits. When Irish immigrants came to America, they started using pumpkins, which were larger and easier to carve.

The Meaning Behind Black Cats

In medieval times, black cats were often associated with witches. Some believed they were witches' companions or even witches in disguise. Today, black cats are considered symbols of luck in some cultures, despite their spooky reputation.

The Largest Pumpkin Ever Grown

The world record for the heaviest pumpkin is over 2,700 pounds. That's heavier than a small car!

Halloween Memories and Writing Prompts

Take a moment to reflect on your favorite Halloween moments. Here are a few prompts to inspire you:

1 What was your most memorable Halloween costume?

2 Did you ever go trick-or-treating as a child? What was your favorite candy to receive?

3 Do you have any Halloween traditions you love?

4 Have you ever had a spooky or funny Halloween experience?

5 What would be your dream Halloween celebration?

Feel free to write your thoughts in the space provided or simply take a moment to reminisce before continuing to color.

Hazel Thorne

Fun Coloring Challenges and Creative Prompts

To make your coloring experience even more engaging, try some of these creative challenges:

- **Limited Palette Challenge**: Choose only three colors and use them to complete an entire page.

- **Spooky Glow Effect**: Use light colors surrounded by dark shades to create an eerie glow.

- **Opposite Colors Experiment**: Try using colors you wouldn't normally associate with Halloween, such as pink and turquoise.

- **Upside-Down Challenge**: Try coloring a page while holding the book upside down to see your design in a new way.

A Final Note

Thank you for bringing these Halloween illustrations to life with your creativity. There is no right or wrong way to color—every page you complete is unique and special. Whether you are coloring for relaxation, fun, or nostalgia, this book is here to provide an enjoyable and stress-free artistic escape.

If you enjoyed this book, consider sharing it with a friend or loved one who might also appreciate the joy of coloring. Your creativity is what makes this book truly special, and I hope you find as much joy in coloring these pages as I did in creating them.

Happy coloring and have a wonderfully spooky Halloween!

xxx  xxx

www.ingramcontent.com/pod-product-compliance
Lightning Source LLC
LaVergne TN
LVHW070216080526
838202LV00067B/6833